DONCASTER'S TRAMS AND TROLLEYBUSES

1902-1963

by
C.T. Goode

Cover Picture:- A view of 1910 looking from Printing Office Street into Station Road

ISBN 1 870 313 16x

Produced by
Burstwick Print & Publicity Services
Hull

Contents

Foreword.

This little work has turned out to be a mixture of reminiscence and factual history in approximately equal measures. It has been a pleasant task to record the public transport scene in Doncaster over the years when it was at its most vigorous, formative and most interesting, before mass popular transport came along in the form of the car. The period under review evokes the older pattern of streets before the ring road came and chopped St. George's church off from the heart of town life.

Unfortunately, I never knew the trams, though my mother did, with her earliest memories being of the tram route along Catherine Street with its passing loop outside the front door, and of the Balby terminus at Oswin Avenue, enriched by the 'last tobacco shop' going out and the 'first tobacco shop' going in, depending on which way the shop sign was read.

My wartime exploits on the tracklesses explain themselves. Incidentally, I cannot remember any sort of metal or wood DCT bus stop sign. Nothing ever offered itself to the young trophy hunter, so I can only assume that travellers had to make do with something stencilled on to a convenient post at the roadside.

Thanks are due to Mrs. C. Hill of the local studies library, Doncaster, for her assistance.

C. T. Goode.
Anlaby 1995.

'A new attraction is added to the show.'

Prior to the arrival of the trams in Doncaster, transport was, as in almost all other commercial centres, provided by horse drawn vehicles, with a number of small operators running from outlying points into the centre of the town. At this focal point in Doncaster, St. Sepulchre Gate was the grocery establishment of Messrs. Hodgson & Hepworth who ran a vehicle which enabled would-be customers to reach their premises more easily, rather in the same way that the modern supermarkets situated out-of-town operate today. The British Electric Company had let it be known that they were interested in laying down a tramway system in Doncaster to link Wheatley Hills in the north east with Balby in the south west, a distance of about four miles by the town centre. This interest shown by an outside body soon roused the Borough Council into activity, and in 1898 they applied for a Light Railway order to provide a tramway system in Doncaster within the town and extending out for quite some distance into the mining community of Bentley, north of the town. At an enquiry at the Mansion House in 1899 an objection was made to this by the Great Northern Railway Company who pointed to the difficulties which a flat crossing of their main line between London and York which would occur north of the station could cause, with its three way junction (the other routes were to Hull and Leeds), station working and a heavy traffic during race meetings. A substantial road bridge, called in its time by an enquiry into the future of Doncaster's transport 'the busiest bridge in South Yorkshire, especially as it carried the A1 main road, was not opened until May 1910, this meaning that the trams appointed to the Bentley route spent their lives until then in isolation on the other side of the railway lines. Power for the tramway was abundant, being supplied by the Corporation from 1899 from its own works adjacent to the brand new depot in Greyfriars Road. The depot was a fine and substantial, light and airy building having the tracks which could house 35 cars set parallel to the roadway outside, the cars turning through a right angle to reach them. Next to the depot were the swimming baths.

The first fifteen cars arrived by rail from Dick, Kerr of Preston in 1902, reaching the Shakespeare Dock yard at the foot of Hexthorpe bridge and being assembled on their wheels at the depot soon after arrival. The trucks upon which they ran were Brill 6ft. 21E type. All of them had reversed stairs and open tops, and a total seating capacity of 56. The trackwork was laid first on the routes to Balby and Hexthorpe in the

No.4 lopes along to the terminus at Hexthorpe Flatts with a full load on the opening day *Doncaster Libraries*

south west, using an unusual centre grooved rail as also found in Hull. These first routes were opened in June 1902 at a time of great rejoicing, not purely because of the dawn of a new era in street transport but because of the ending of the Boer war at that time.

The Chairman of the Tramways Committee was Councillor George Smith, a Retford man by birth who began his career with Messrs. Hodgson & Hepworth, noted grocer's in St. Sepulchre Gate. His aspirations led him to buy the mineral water business of Mr. Heath who had recently died, cementing the union by marrying the latter's eldest daughter. The firm of Heath & Smith became well known in the town and the name is still prominent today.

On Monday 2nd June a procession of notables left the Mansion House at 1.45pm. from the Electric Power station and, as noted, the whole town was in jovial mood with the ending of the war, in fact the Great Northern Railway works and wagon repair shops were in the throes of a day's holiday for the occasion. The outdoor assembly was very noisy, to such an extent that only Alderman F. Clark was able to make himself heard, with the greatest din marking patriotic remarks rather than local politics. Councillor Smith presented the Mayor, Thos. Windle with an 18 carat gold key topped by a crown set with the town coat of arms. The Chairman of the Electrical Committee, Councillor Dawson, presented Councillor Smith with a gold model controller handle in the form of a watch pendant, while Mr. Beaton for the suppliers of the rolling stock, Messrs. Dick, Kerr, not to be outshone, presented the Mayoress and Mrs. Smith with miniature silver plated and ebony control handles. One wonders if the firm kept a supply of these trinkets to dole out at other places where their tramcars were bought.

Hustle and bustle in Station Road with a Hexthorpe car leaving and one arriving from Avenue Road　　　　　　　　　　　　*Doncaster Libraries*

Two routes were ready, to Balby (Hall Flatt Lane) and Hexthorpe (Flatts); these had been duly inspected and passed muster by Major Druitt and Mr. Trotter. A visit to Hull had been of interest and led to the adoption of the centre grooved rail, though this was set in concrete and not, as with Hull, in wood. The total length of the system would be essentially some nine miles and cost £77,500. It was intended that the Flatts at Hexthorpe would be an eventual draw for passengers when it was developed as a public park.

The trams set off with the Mayoress and Mr. Wyld, the Corporation's Electrical engineer driving the first car laden with the Mayor and retinue, while the second was driven by Geo. Smith accompanied by the Tramway Committee. A third car was filled with invited guests. Some 700-800 pinafores were given away to any ladies with children who had bought tram tickets on the day. Each car was decorated with flags at each end, while on the Grand Theatre in Station Road a banner was displayed with 'Success to the Corporation Trams' thereon.

The first day's takings were £43.19s.5d. for an estimated 10,553 passengers carried, who paid, though hundreds availed themselves of free rides, overwhelming the conductors. On the Tuesday £34.3s. was collected, though things had calmed by the Wednesday morning, always a slack period, when each car carried an average of 20 passengers.

Details in the above are from the local 'Gazette' of the period. A more subjective and perhaps cynical review of events is given in the 'Chronicle' to be found at the end of this work.

The next route to be completed was the double tracked Race Course route at the end of June. Normally fairly quiet during the year, the moderately short run with its terminus by the stands in Grand Stand Road would work all-out during September Race Week, when almost the whole town would visit the course for a flutter. During the September race period in the first year of operation, all but two cars were used on the service to ferry punters to the course.

The awkwardly situated Bentley route was also opened in 1902, and the four isolated trams were housed in a converted stable until the railway bridge was opened in 1910. After this, routes to Avenue Road to serve the Infirmary on Thorne Road, Beckett Road in the same north easterly direction and to Oxford Street were inaugurated. The latter was

No. 24 in the wilder parts of the Bentley route. Note the roof canopy and conductress.   *Doncaster Libraries*

a short run and was closed in less than two years as the terminus was within walking distance of the town centre. Takings were minimal on this curiosity of a route.

Sunday services were not developed until 1914 and then probably as a result of the wartime atmosphere with the need also for men to travel between the station and Glasgow Paddocks in Waterdale to and from leave.

A summary of opening dates for the tramway routes is as follows:

Balby cum Hexthorpe	2/6/1902
Race Course	30/6/1902
Hyde Park	1/8/1902
Bentley	27/10/1902
Frenchgate	27/10/1902
Avenue Road	15/1/1903
Beckett Road	17/8/1903
Oxford Street	25/11/1903
Brodsworth	21/2/1916

With the opening of the bridge over the railway in 1911 the Bentley trams were 'liberated' and ran through into Frenchgate to a point outside Guildhall. The bridge also carried a further route, a long one out to the mining village of Woodlands, called erroneously Brodsworth, though no doubt with the nearby colliery in mind. This was an interesting run of four miles, mainly on reserved track with eleven passing places on the single line which came into use in February 1916 at about the same time as the Hull & Barnsley and Great Central Joint railway line came to the area with the terminal station layout at York Road in the fork of the Brodsworth and Bentley routes. It was more than likely the trams which caused the station to remain incomplete and unused by any passengers. The line provided a further bridge for the A1 and the Brodsworth route to cross. On the opening of the latter the Bentley cars joined it in terminating round the corner at the foot of North Bridge in Trafford Street.

In 1903-4 ten further cars were purchased which were identical to the first fifteen and which took the numbers 16-25. Of these, the 'special' car was No. 21 which was the vehicle decorated for special festivals and which achieved a kind of glory by being the last open topper in service.

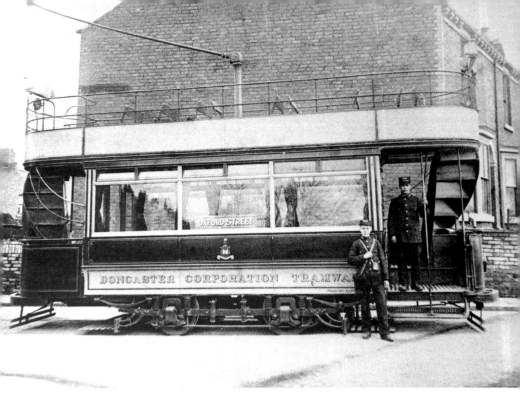

A car on the short lived Oxford Street route. *Doncaster Libraries*

At this time the Corporation had three interesting service vehicles, a horse drawn tower wagon which lasted up to the Great War, a salt and sand trailer which was a conversion from a York vehicle, and a powered snow broom car on a standard 6ft. Brill truck. Both the latter survived to the demise of trams in the town. In 1912 a chain driven Albion tower wagon was purchased to replace the horse drawn vehicle; though the rest of the car was sold to a Sheffield dealer, the tower portion was to last for many years afterwards.

For a time before the Great War cross town running evolved and was operated by cars working from Avenue Road-Hexthorpe and Beckett Road-Balby. This was discontinued after a time because of the problems which are often encountered with this method, such as late running on the second leg due to delay on the first and to a greater passenger demand on one route than another. Such matters are more easily solved by a turn-round in the town centre. An extension of the Balby route from Oswin Avenue to Warmsworth beyond the town boundary was carried out in 1915.

A view of 1910 looking from Printing Office Street into Station Road, where the heart of the tramway system was situated.   Coll: C.T. Goode

Doncaster at this period enjoyed the unenviable reputation of being the sootiest spot in South Yorks. and this led to the next batch of cars delivered by Dick, Kerr in 1913, also 56 seaters, having roofs on the cars Nos. 26-31 running on Peckham 7ft.6in. P22 trucks. Passengers on the Balby route were able to enjoy the new vehicles which worked almost exclusively on that service. No. 32 was an odd car of 74 seats running on a 13ft.6in. radial truck. 'Big Ben', as the car was affectionately known, was wont to derail on curved sections and so its long wheelbase was shortened to an 8ft.6in. Peckham P35 bogie. Many of the earlier cars except Nos. 1-4 and 17-21 were fitted with top deck covers and direct stairs like the later ones during 1913. In some cases the wheelbase was lengthened in the hope of giving a smoother ride, in the event this did not reduce the jarring but alleviated the sensation of proceeding on a storm-tossed sea. Possibly money was not available for total conversion and improvements, and only four of the cars had provision made on the lower deck for non-smokers by the use of a partition.

In 1916 four further cars, Nos. 33-36 were purchased from Dick, Kerr, these being unvestibuled balcony cars with direct stairs on Peckham 8ft.6in trucks. They were provided for the new Brodsworth route.

The final set of new cars, Nos. 38-47 were not really required when they arrived at Greyfriars Road in 1920, as the Corporation were already bothered by a loss of income and a generally run-down system, due to lack of maintenance. Already, too, the motor bus was making its presence felt locally in the beginnings of several private operators who, having bought redundant WD vehicles, would ply for years to come as far as Rossington, Armthorpe, Hatfield and Thorne, to which places it was hoped that eventually the new cars would run. By the Second World War these operators had been allocated stopping places around Christ Church on Thorne Road, where it was possible to view some vintage rolling stock and equally veteran drivers.

The latter batch of cars had 66 seats, vestibules and balconies, running on Peckham P22 trucks. They were the only cars to have enclosed platforms. No. 40 was the last tram in service in the town in June 1935.

Not very inspiring view of St. Sepulchre Gate around 1910 with a tram in the distance and a good view of the overhead.   *Coll: C.T. Goode*

DONCASTER. ST SEPULCHRE GATE

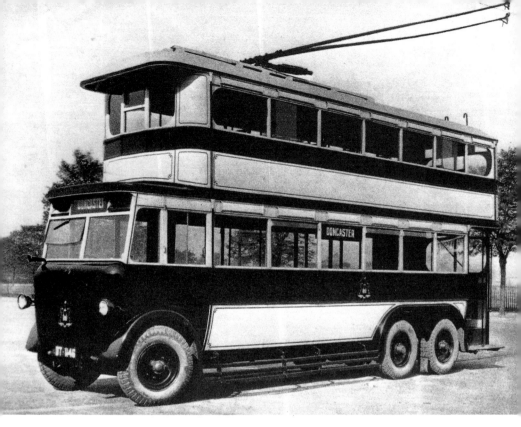

One of the new trolley buses, No.8 poses, most likely at the racecourse
soon after delivery Doncaster Libraries

Probably the most intriguing of all the Corporation electric vehicles was the one about which least is known, No. 37 of 1917 which was purchased secondhand from Erith UDC in Kent (their No. 15) and used for its short life of a year on the Avenue Road route. It was described as a 'demicar' on which the driver collected fares at the front end, with seating for 14, a 5ft.6in. Mountain & Gibson truck and regenerative brakes. There were a few of these little cars about, as at Glossop and Chester. History did repeat itself with the Corporation's acquisition of five Seddon 'Midibuses', all of which had a somewhat longer life than No. 37, running on a town circular service in the 70's, noisy in operation and odd and amusing to look at.

The tramway layout at Doncaster was of the simplest, being basically single track except on the Race Course route and at certain points in the town centre. There were nine passing loops on the Balby route after a run of double track up to Balby Bridge, and standage for two cars side by side at Warmsworth. Hexthorpe had two loops, Hyde Park had one in Catherine Street - this route was, unlike the later trolley bus one, out and home to Carr House Road. Beckett Road and Wheatley Hills (Avenue Road) had a passing loop each, while Bentley was well supplied with seven. As the longest route, Brodsworth managed eleven passing places on its run of mainly reserved track to the west of the roadway. Cars at the outer end of the Race Course route could turn by means of a circle in Grand Stand Road.

As the new trolley buses came along, withdrawal of the trams went on apace in the twenties and early thirties, the first route, to Avenue Road being abandoned on 25th April 1925 with an almost total conversion to trolleybuses resulting by 1931, except for the Brodsworth route which soldiered on until 1935 when it was then converted directly to motor bus operation, these departing from Trafford Street in the same manner as the trams. Withdrawal of the trams occurred as follows:

1927	Nos. 1-5, 17-20.
1929	No. 21 (last open topper).
1930	Nos. 6-16, 22-25.
1931	Nos. 26-30, 32.
1932	Nos. 31, 33, 35.
1933	Nos. 34, 36, 38, 41.
1935	Nos. 39, 40, 42, 43-47.

The last to go ended their days on the Brodsworth route and became a sorry sight. During its last month or so of operation No. 40 distinguished itself by burning itself out due to an electrical fault while on service.

Much maligned and always intriguing, with that air of superiority which all trams seemed to have, the days of the tram in Doncaster were, alas, numbered and the last car ran in June 1935, leaving a deficit of £168,000 which would be recouped by the new trolley vehicles.

Motor vehicles purchased after the 1914-18 War were set to work on new routes to Skellow, Edlington, Rossington and Stainforth. Petrol vehicles were also put on to the Avenue Road tram route which was not extended to Wheatley Hills. After deliberation the Transport Committee and Mr. Tommy Potts, the Manager, decided to go ahead with the adoption of trolley vehicles within the borough, this in the light of the performance of the petrol vehicles on the Wheatley Hills run, which tended to be heavy on fuel, due in part to the high number of stops on a short run. Here, of course, the prime arguments in favour of trolley buses could come into their own; the quietness, ease of acceleration and deceleration and use of the 'home grown' electricity in Greyfriars Road.

New 'tracklesses' and conversions.

In the year after Doncaster became a County Borough, the first trolleybuses appeared on the streets. These were always known as tracklesses, or 'trackies' locally, and the first of them arrived during 1928. Nos. 1-4 were Garretts, Nos. 5-8 Karriers and all were fitted with double rear axles. As Doncaster arrived somewhat later in the trolleybus field than most companies, the manufacturers were able to come up with something solid and relatively handsome, with 60 seats and a fine rake of six downstairs and seven upstairs windows, the upper deck stepped back to leave a single storey driving cab except for a capuchon of projecting roof at the front, under which was the destination number box. The livery was a sort of magnolia relieved by two maroon bands, the broader one around the waistline running to the cab area whose sides and front were totally maroon. To the author this early livery, which persisted on the vehicles throughout wartime, was reminiscent of the blood and fattiness of a butcher's shop.

No. 1 began trials and training on the adapted Race Course route, using the positive overhead wire and a skate return to the rail. The Bentley route was the first to be converted by the specialists in overhead wiring, Messrs. Clough, Smith on 21st. August 1928 and was a fairly easy job of double wiring with some single poles and brackets on Bentley Road and one bridge to pass under near the Don Bridge. This No. 1 route was extended into a circular run round Bentley New village and ran to a new annex at the town side of the North Bridge, a reason not readily obvious, as the vehicles could just as easily run on into town, halt

No.1 on trials with one trolley arm raised to the tram wire and a skate earth rail; tram No. 7 is alongside, ostensibly on the Race Course route. The picture was probably taken in the town centre.   Coll: C.T. Goode

in one of the quieter streets and run outward through Trafford Street. The terminus chosen gave vehicles a nasty start on the outward run by having to cross southbound traffic on the A1, plus having to filter in to that going in the opposite direction. It is surprising that such a manoeuvre lasted as long as it did; in fairness, with the system as it existed, arriving vehicles could slip into the platform quite smartly.

Next to be converted was the Hexthorpe route in July 1929 (No.3), a short run with a 1/2d. fare to a turning circle opposite the Dell, which was a pretty park offering lovers' walks, rockeries, putting, boating on the river and fine display of illuminated tableaux in the autumn, all of which was good revenue fodder. Most people, however, especially the courting couples, would choose to walk out to there. This route was really an offshoot of the principal route to Balby and Warnsworth. Probably due to lack of sufficient money, this longer route was not converted until July 1931 and then only to Austen Avenue (No. 10), the last road on the Corporation estate into which buses turned to use a reverser, which was a T shape. The vehicle would run into the left arm, the trolley booms clearing spring points in the overhead wires which would now enable the vehicle to run backwards across into the right arm over a second set of spring points which would now be set in their normal position for the run down the body of the T, that is back down Austen Avenue to the main road.

Warmsworth was really outside the town boundary and an intensified motor bus service to Edlington, plus Yorkshire Traction and Rotherham Corporation services from Conisbrough and beyond catered for the village which was of no great size. It was during the second War in 1942, that the Balby route was extended almost to the boundary at Barrel Lane, where a turning circle was installed to create a similar problem to that at North Bridge, namely causing turning vehicles to cross one lot of heavy traffic before having to filter into another. The local outcry against the extension was great, as it was feared that the buses would be filled up on setting out by Edlington miners in their 'pit muck', who had walked up from Yorkshire Main colliery. In the event, very few miners appeared, having their own motor bus 'specials'.

No.14 passes along St Sepulchre Gate on an inbound service. Morris's wallpaper shop to the left. 'Sammy' Morris became Mayor at one time.
Photo: W.J. Haynes

The Beckett Road run (No.5) was converted at about the same time as the Balby service, being extended to a reverser at Wentworth Road, and by a further half a mile in 1941. In Nether Hall Road division took place between the latter route and that to Avenue Road which was extended to a turning circle in front of the Wheatley hotel, along Thorne Road. Eventually another park, Sandall Park, was opened near here to create further revenue. Avenue Road, being narrow, had a neat row of single arm bracket supports carrying the two pairs of wires for both directions along its straight and gently rising length, one of the most impressive sections of overhead in the town. The Wheatley Hills route (No.4) serving what was certainly perhaps the most desirable residential area at the time, had to wait until March 1931 before conversion.

Trams were retained on the reserved track of the Brodsworth route until 1935 before conversion to motor buses.

Obviously more trolleybuses were needed to operate the converted system than the original eight acquired, and so a further 22 three axle Karriers, Nos. 9-30 were supplied in three lots to 1931. One of the first eight, No. 8, was borrowed for trials in Nottingham for a time, and No. 22 travelled overseas to South Africa as a demonstrator for a few months.

The odd one out in the fleet at this time was No. 31 of 1929, though outwardly similar to the earlier vehicles and having a Roe body, was in fact built on a Bristol motor bus chassis adapted for trolleybus use, one of two isolated experiments put in hand by a firm normally occupied with motor bus work. Possibly some sort of challenge had been offered to Messrs. Chas. H. Roe, which had been readily taken up.

No. 32 was, in many ways, one of the most famous or notorious of the Doncaster trolleybus fleet, and became of course senior member on the scrapping of the earlier vehicles after the 1939-45 War. Originally designed to Mr. T. Pott's specifications, No. 32 was used as demonstrator by Karriers and Roe and it was always duly respected for this, enthusiasts being told that parts underneath were chrome plated. They never quite believed this and never glimpsed any gleaming areas; however, they were ready to accept the fact and to allow the old bus a moment or two of glory. In later years it ran almost exclusively on the Bentley route with a fine dent in the front offside, the number blind obstinately fixed on '3' (Hexthorpe) instead of the required '1'.

Nos. 33-36 were identical to No. 32, apart from the dent, and came along in 1935, two years later. These four spent their latter days on the Bentley route. The intermediate series of 1930's vintage trolleybuses came next, Nos. 37-42, six further vehicles of improved outline, especially at the front end taking to the road in 1937. At this time all the various ages of vehicles were to be found on the system.

The fleet is established.

Eventually, in 1937 came the first batch of vehicles, Nos. 43-8 which could be considered as the most typical and most aesthetically pleasing of the Doncaster trolleybus fleet. These had the improved H6OR body with a high domed roof and full rounded front, whereas the previous ones had been slightly angular, quite up-to-date in appearance when compared with some of the apparitions running around in Nottingham or Derby, and quite acceptable up to the time for scrapping

An unidentified vehicle on the Hyde Park route at Clock Corner.
Coll: C.T. Goode

Clock Corner and Baxter Gate Doncaster.

in the 1950's. Like the livery sported by No.32, the accent was now on a chestnut maroon with grey roof and three bands of off-white round the vehicle below the upper windows and above and below the lower ones, the lowest band being broader and taking in the front side lights. Between the upper and lower decks was the destination indicator which had the route number printed in above, integral with the destination name. Low on the side body flank was the town coat of arms with motto, no doubt chosen with the vehicles in mind: 'Confort et Liesse'. The final batch of twenty similar vehicles came to the town in 1939, Nos. 49-68 and so the fleet remained until inroads were made on the earlier vehicles and the balance was restored by purchasing two axle utility vehicles in 1943.

No. 16 passes the bank in High Street. Note the early form of livery with cream lower stripes.   Coll: C.T. Goode

Disposition of the vehicles is quite interesting, even though it does involve a test of memory. During the early part of the war the oldest vehicles were to be found on the Bentley route, sharing runs with Nos. 32-6. As mentioned, No. 32 spent much time on this route. The Hyde Park and Race Course circulars which ran counter to each other attracted vehicles from the No. 37-48 group, though these were also seen on the Beckett Road service. Balby enjoyed the latest rolling stock, Nos.49-68 and some of them ran on the route more or less all their days. Rarely indeed did one see one of the older Karriers on the Balby run; these were chosen to work the Hexthorpe and Wheatley Hills routes exclusively for quite a time, this quirk persisting when wartime replacements arrived to take their place. Demarcation of the Hexthorpe and Balby routes in wartime was almost total, and it was just as unlikely to ride up to Balby on an old Karrier as it was to sail over Hexthorpe Bridge on No.68. The reasons for this are obscure, unless the indicator blinds were immovable. Having said that, however, it is noteworthy that the Karrier vehicles had their destination blinds with 'Hexthorpe' and 'Wheatley Hills' printed through in red, more than likely to assist the employee at night to change the points in the overhead for the correct route.

Wartime memories.

The scene is now set for my own great exploits on board the Doncaster trolleybuses during my wartime travels to the Grammar School, to and fro between there and Balby, twice a day for six days a week, as we went on Saturdays, even in wartime! My experiences will always keep trolleybuses as something special for the rest of my life. I had a good tally of fast ten minute trips and a frequent headway of five minutes or so, the new vehicles giving a solid and reliable run. During the war period the vehicles had netting stuck to the windows to reduce the effects of possible bomb blast, and lighting was of course masked to provide the minimum. Each vehicle was equipped with loudspeakers downstairs rear and upstairs front so that the driver could announce the stops in the blackout, it being assumed that he would certainly know where he was! This was a dubious success as the squeaking and vibration lent a peculiarly ghostly atmosphere to the driver's rendering of 'Balby Bridge' and 'Fairway'. With a keen ear one could also enjoy sundry swearing as the driver vented his feelings on other road users, or singing if the mood were different.

Nos.26 and 27 pass each other at Oswin Avenue Balby on the first day of operation, 26/7/1931. In the last weeks the trains had run using the inner of each of the pairs of new overhead wires. In the Balby route 6 vehicles were used on weekdays with 13 on Saturdays, each taking 12 minutes outward and 13 minutes return.   Doncaster Libraries

There was no doubt that, in wartime the combination of fog often encountered and blackout did far more harm than even the Germans could manage, bringing road traffic rapidly to a halt. In these days before the word 'pollution' was discovered, fogs really were thick and yellow in colour, while visibility really was nil. Often, however, the 'trackies' would struggle on, only to grind to a halt en route and be abandoned at the roadside until things improved. It was well-nigh impossible to manoeuvre a bus into the correct position under the overhead points at Hexthorpe bridge, for example, when turning off across the road. A dewirement was a disaster in such conditions; there would be ominous twanging and bumping noises from on high, the lights would go out and of course we would stop. The bamboo pole would be drawn out from under the rear of the bus, by the driver as a rule, though he sometimes waited to see if the conductor would jump to it first. He would fish about aloft until he retrieved the errant boom-no retrieving wires on DCT! This chore was especially the drivers' during the war period, when conductresses were employed in great numbers. It was not unknown

No. 332 is seen at the North Bridge Terminus of the Bentley route. This vehicle, the first of the new series, worked almost exclusively on this route.
C.T. Goode

for a lady of slender proportions to be lifted up in the air like a Clochemerle bellringer when the tension springs on the booms proved too much for her. It was, however, a conductress who, at Carr Hill on the Balby route one night, after her bus had dewired at a particularly fierce and notorious isolating gap festooned with feeder cables and jumpers, got out and adroitly re-connected the booms to the overhead, or so she thought. No lights came on, though, nor did anything else. Finally the driver emerged from the cab, came round behind and soon discovered that his enthusiastic companion had in fact connected the left hand boom to a street lighting wire running parallel alongside.

There were some real characters as trolleybus drivers in those days, the old boys dawdled along and wore heavy regulation coats even in the hottest weather, the vaguely criminal looking types dressed in any sort of civvy gear who would drive with head permanently turned to admire the lasses in the front seats behind them; the foot jabbers who, on leaving a stop with great panache, continually brought out the circuit breakers with frightening flashes and who would then stand up and fish about wildly above their heads to restore the current. And there was Adolph. We schoolboys were convinced that it was the Führer himself, for there he sat uncannily always in charge of our bus, be it No.61 (my favourite), 63 or 68, heavily great-coated and always in his regulation Corporation peaked cap, beneath which were two beady eyes and The Moustache. He never seemed to emerge and say a word to anyone, just drove smoothly along. He certainly fascinated me during an impressionable time. I wonder whatever happened to him?

I have just mentioned the isolating gap. These were at places where feeder wires came in, and at each it was possible to isolate a section or take current from the nearby section by a through switch. They were always obvious by the clutter of insulators and wiring which attended them-even today they are to be seen clearly on the new Sheffield tramway system-and also by the distinctive thud as the trolley arms passed through them. On the Balby route they were in evidence at the foot of Hexthorpe Bridge, Carr Hill and Oswin Avenue.

The trolleybus extended its influence to other places as well as Balby. The route to Hexthorpe cost only 1d and not 2d. and had the older vehicles with fronts like upright pianos, which had to wait subserviently for us superior Balby folk, so we thought, at the foot of Hexthorpe Bridge. This was in actual fact because the Balby service stood in front of the Hexthorpe one at the terminus in West Laith Gate. If a Balby bus were in sight, it was sense to wait for it. The wires at the foot of the bridge tailed in, ran parallel for a short way and then converged, the Balby wires doglegging into the Hexthorpe. One morning I was fascinated to observe, as we rolled down Balby Bridge, that the Hexthorpe vehicle was waiting as usual, but was on the town side of the points, all in blissful ignorance Would our driver notice? He did not. We sailed past. There was a terrific booming and cracking overhead, every wire in sight bounced up and down and our vehicle suffered a broken boom. The now incapacitated vehicle was moved to the side of the road by means of the conductor touching the wire with the broken stub of boom.

The older Karriers had the red destination blinds for the Wheatley Hills and Hexthorpe indications, along with red 3s. or 4s. in the number boxes. They were pleasant to ride in, solid and with a comfortable aroma of tobacco smoke about the leather seats upstairs, no doubt

No.32 at North Bridge, Complete with dent.   *C.T. Goode*

because of the lack of ventilation. 'No Spitting' was the written command as well. Downstairs the seats were in a pinky moquette and workmen and   miners were discouraged from travelling below in no uncertain terms. Downstairs, smoking was confined to the rear. Upstairs on the Bentley route, the air in winter was of a thick blue colour, due to Thick Twist and Woodbines.

It was easy to change the indicator blinds from the front seats upstairs on the older vehicles, as the handles were in tempting positions, so that 'Depot' appeared many times when it shouldn't have. The old Karriers were impressive in their maroon with plenty of cream, and delightful with their long strings running the length of each deck to work the starting and stopping bell somewhere in the cab. The driver possessed a large bulb horn and, by the cab doors on each side a couple of deadly weapons in the form of white painted wooden arrows with a red blob, both pointing upwards. On turning, the driver would let one fall to indicate his direction, deadly indeed for any cyclist; they would descend just at head height!

Minimal gear, efficient operation.

Considering that Doncaster's trolleybuses ran on seven routes, it was something of a feat for only four overhead points to be used at the only two double junctions, namely where the Beckett Road route left that to Wheatley Hills, and where the Hexthorpe route parted company with the Balby Route. The facing points at the latter junction were always slightly risky in operation, even latterly when actuated by the usual skate ahead of them; thus, one would have the somewhat alarming experience of sitting upstairs with the bus making for Balby Bridge, while seeing the booms doing their best to make for Hexthorpe until being brought from the wires when at full stretch, to swing round and shatter the upper windows of the handy YMCA Tea Rooms. At the crossing place of the two sets of wires was a heavy and primitive looking device which, I am certain, was originally a couple of blocks of wood with the wires stapled on beneath-the vehicle's passing gave that impression!

No.358 drops off a passenger at Waverley Avenue.   *C.T. Goode*

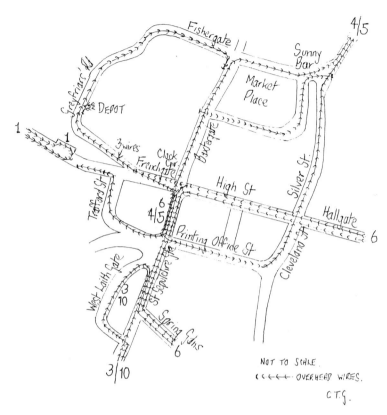

Other pointwork there was, including a surprisingly efficient reverser system at the end of Balby route up to around 1942, before the extension to Barrel Lane. The other couple of points, and the Freak was one of them, were part of a fascinating set of knitwear used to bring vehicles from the depot in Greyfriars Road to their respective routes. To appreciate this, the diagram should be studied. The Bentley route was always independent, its wiring being continuous and with the town terminus based in a concrete lay-by on the side of North Bridge. To emerge, vehicles had to turn across both lanes of traffic, a great difficulty on busy Saturdays. It will be seen from the plan how trolleybuses were run round to the Bentley route from the depot, up past the police station in Frenchgate to Clock Corner over a weird section with three wires as far as the Freak, a point on the middle wire which divided it into two, this now making two sets of wires, one of

No.346 waits at the foot of Hexthorpe Bridge as a Balby service runs past into the town. It's a Sunday in 1948.   C.T. Goode

which ran straight on through a trailing point into the Race Course route at Baxter Gate end, a route which was circular and otherwise attached to nothing else. The other set of wires came round from Frenchgate into St. Sepulchre Gate on the wrong side of the road, and vehicles for the Bentley route proceeded in this unorthodox way round into Trafford Street and round the corner towards North Bridge where they were connected to the Bentley route. On this system a vehicle missed picking up at its terminus, and would have to sally forth on its journey empty. Buses coming off the route were run wrong side of the road (the A1!) into Trafford Street, a most laboured effort, though downhill.

Buses for the Balby and Hexthorpe routes could be sent right round the Race Course circuit to meet up with the inbound wires on the north side of St. Sepulchre Gate, with which the Race Course overhead ran parallel here: this was a long, 'dead' run, and what normally happened was that they would come round like the Bentley vehicles wrong side into St. Sep. as far as Hodgson & Hepworth's, where the booms would then be 'anchored' and would drift across into West Laith Gate or be manhandled across by a bunch of inspectors, staff and anyone interested. This transfer movement could be tricky if it took place on a Saturday lunchtime, say, when traffic was heavy. Vehicles for the Hyde Park route, which was the Race Course circular in reverse, were run wrong side as above, but were then brought across to the right side of

St. Sep. and then transferred to the correct wires outside the Three Legs hotel.

Plenty of manual transfers took place during Race Week in September, when the whole fleet was active bringing in townsfolk, after which, at a given time, most trolleybuses were moved on to the Race Course service to ferry the crowds down to the scene of events. The normally peaceful service became very profitable and the queues to return afterwards were immense. While the trolleybuses were absent, motor buses were used on other routes for the afternoon.

The remaining routes to Wheatley Hills and Beckett Road enjoyed a different means of receiving their motive power, by means of a line of wires which left the depot in the opposite direction running round Fishergate to the Market Place. This link turned for a short way into Baxtergate, and vehicles coming off duty from the Balby, Hexthorpe, Race Course, Wheatley Hills and Beckett Road routes would transfer to the No.4 and 5 wiring down Baxtergate and run to the depot via Fishergate. This leaves the Hyde Park vehicles which returned to depot by running from Hallgate into Cleaveland St., to reconnect with the overhead wires there and follow Wheatley Hills procedure.

From Sunny Bar an unconnected stretch of overhead wire ran round the Market area to a point near to Poynter's butchers in Baxtergate, to enable the No.4 and 5 routes to terminate short of the busy A1 in High Street which they had to cross twice during Race Week. This link was used during 1938 when Baxtergate was closed due to a serious fire involving Messrs. Woolworth's and other shops on 6th May 1938.

The Balby stop in West Laith Gate with No.357. Behind it is one of the wartime purchases on the Hexthorpe service.   C.T. Goode

No.376 takes the Hexthorpe route over the points near the YMCA 'Public Refreshment Rooms'.   *C.T. Goode*

Matters technical.

A brief mention of the more technical aspects of the system is in order. Compared with the wiring arrangements aloft in such places as Bradford and Nottingham, that at Doncaster was very rudimentary, there being latterly the five major points, or 'frogs' to serve all routes. Originally the turn-offs for Hexthorpe and Beckett Road would be manually operated from a stirrup mounted on a convenient post, then, just prior to the 1939 war electric operation was put in, with the driver able to alter the point setting for the branch by passing beneath a skate while drawing power. On the Doncaster system a skate on the branch wire beyond the point restored the point to the main route, when activated under power. The voltage at which the vehicles worked was 550 and each vehicle drew some 3,000 watts under load. The wires were of cadmium copper of Ω section in order to be clamped beneath the span wires. Many of these, especially on the Bentley route, were refurbished tram hangers paired off, the common oval type looking somewhat like a pair of eyebrows spaced apart by an insulation bead. On the Bentley route the wires were set closer together than on other routes; this was possibly verging on the illegal, but being out of town would not be so easily noticed by sharp eyes! In some locations a simpler, more modern span

In 393 in St. Sepulchre Gate rests between runs on the Racecourse route. The trolley arms have been transferred to the depot wiring to be clear of the Wheatley Hills Services, the wiring for which is the centre of the three sets seen here.   C.T.Goode

hanger was used. As on all systems, the live, positive wire was towards the centre of the road, the negative seven feet from the kerb. This latter was theory, as wiring seemed to run closer, as with the depot wiring at Station Road corner and at certain places elsewhere. Minimum height of wiring was 20 ft., this was less at one time in St. Sepulchre Gate where, outside Messrs. Taylor & Colbridge's bookshop, the Nos. 4 and 5 routes crossed the No. 6 by a shallow crossing which looked as if it had long wooden insulators and which rose and fell alarmingly as vehicles navigated it. One way or another there was quite an amount of potential danger literally in the air in trolleybus days, with the risk of falling wires and the attendant span hangers, each of which weighed 3-lb. A dewirement could cause the trolley head to break off. Originally, and until during the war these comprised 31b. bronze pulleys in gun metal swivelling sockets. Each had a retaining loop to keep it with the boom if it parted company, but unfortunately this did not always happen. Many would puzzle as to how the arms ever kept to the wires; this of course happened through the pressure caused by springs on the roof which produced some 40lb. each, greatest when the booms were anchored down, which often proved the undoing of those wartime lady conductors, in fact the similar problem used to face the ladies who drove the Blackpool trams, and who perhaps still do. The trolley wheels were noisy and give the lie to the idea that these vehicles were silent in operation. Especially in summer its swish could be heard through the open windows upstairs as one went along, with whistling noises at times when the overhead wires were angled round curves. During wartime at about the time when the utility vehicles were brought into use, the heads were replaced by carbon sliders about three of four inches long in a metal holder. These reduced noise considerably, along with wear on the wiring, but they needed regular changing.

Post-war developments.

After what seemed a long period of stability; actually it was only four years which was made to appear longer by the war, three further trolleybuses appeared on the streets, two axles models, Nos.69-71 with Karrier chassis and utility Park Royal 56 seater bodies containing seats removed from vehicles withdrawn earlier. These buses were at first painted grey, though with the coat of arms applied, and went into service on the Hexthorpe and Wheatley Hills routes, where they were a success. In 1945 the last of the 1928 Karriers were replaced by six more

No. 334 awaiting dispersal at Leicester Avenue, with dented front end.
Coll: C.T. Goode

two axle vehicles which became Nos. 72-77. The first of the batch, three, were Brush bodied in grey, the latter three were Park Royal bodied in chocolate livery, all utility. The vehicles had leather seats which spared passengers the more acute horror of sitting on wooden slatting which was to be found on some of the motor vehicles owned by the Corporation and the Yorkshire Traction utility models.

In the early post-war period, therefore, DCT had a fleet of 46 trolley vehicles operating on seven routes, the lightest being the Race Course and Hyde Park circulars which could well manage on a couple of vehicles each in slack periods. The most popular run would be that to Balby with a steady flow of passengers on and off at each stop. The fare for the through run was 2d. (blue ticket) for many years with 1½d. (white) being charged to Balby Church and 1d. (buff) for children over any distance. Weekly passes for the whole run entitled the holder to four daily journeys end to end at 2/6d. (12½p.) (blue) and 2/- (10p.) (white) to Balby Church only. Each pass was about 3" x 2" and had the journey units printed round the edges for clipping as used. Saturday was a busy day for the unscrupulous who would turn over the litter bins and gutters to find discarded passes with unused journeys left thereon which could be used up as part of a night out. Scholars' free passes were in the form of a neat opening folder in leather cloth, red for two journeys each day using two routes, black for two journeys on a single route only.

Before Mr. Potts retired in 1953 replacements were obtained for ageing No.s 32-6, these being ex Darlington BUT East Lancs. bodied two axle vehicles, again with 56 seats. They became Nos. 378-83, the prefix 3 having appeared around 1948 to make clear the trolley vehicles from the motor buses. The livery was now slightly different, there being but one white band above the lower deck. The numbers were also given a plainer form without serifs and shading.

The new transport manager was Mr. Bamford, who came from Maidstone, and the following year after his arrival it was decided to rebody the nine utility vehicles, Nos. 369-77 with 62 seater Roe bodies, though No. 370 was not converted at that time. Further vehicles were purchased from Southend-on-Sea (Nos. 130-8) which were again two axle, nine in all and utility Karrier with Park Royal bodies, except for one Brush product. These became Nos. 384-92 and ran in the place of earlier vehicles which were scrapped. To an enthusiast, coping with transfers of vehicles can become quite a complicated business, and DCT

No.363 heads into town at the foot of Hexthorpe Bridge. The Hexthorpe wiring converges at the points, while on the other side can be seen the overhead skate to change the points for the other direction.

C.T. Goode

shopped around fairly considerably for secondhand rolling stock which was probably on the market cheaply. From their nearest neighbours, the Mexborough & Swinton Traction Company, they bought Sunbeam single deckers Nos. 1-6 which were then rebodied with the now obligatory Roe 62 seat body and took Nos. 393-98 in 1955.

In spite of this rash of new acquisitions it was now becoming obvious that the Doncaster trolleybus was now reaching the end of its useful days. Certainly the old six wheeler Karriers were being pensioned off in increasing numbers, with 34 coming off the road in early 1956, the principal cause being the conversion to motor bus of the Bentley route at that time. By July 1957 only four of the older Karriers were left, Nos 364, 366, 367 and 368. Then, on 29th September 1957 Nos. 367-8 made final runs as last survivors of their type. Acquisitions were still being made, however, the penultimate being in the form of Karriers with Weymann utility bodies from Pontypridd. When rebodied by Roe they became Nos. 351-2, taking up older trolleybus numbers. The very last to appear were Mexborough & Swinton Nos. 14 and 18 similar in form to Nos. 1-6 which were rebuilt in the same way and given Nos. 353-4.

With the often confusing logic of local authorities in general and often of British Rail in the past, a few years before scrapping two new extensions to the Beckett Road and Wheatley Hills routes were opened in February and October 1958 respectively. During the fifties too, the older maroon and cream livery had been 'improved' to a more reddish hue and less cream was in evidence, except for a single band above the lower windows.

The end is nigh.

In November 1961 it was announced that the trolleybuses would be gradually withdrawn from the town, due to road improvements, the bane of such systems everywhere, except perhaps in Europe, where progress seems to cope with both trolleys and trams quite well. As mentioned, the Bentley route had gone in 1956, due to the replacement of a bridge over the Don. In 1961 there were still 28 vehicles left as follows:

369-71. 372-74. 375-77. 384-86.
38792. 393-95. 396-98. 351-52.
353-54.

A group of vehicles awaits scrapping at Leicester Avenue depot. The only identifiable vehicle is third from the right, No.340 with separate name and number blinds.   *Coll: C.T. Goode*

Following the demise of the Bentley route, the next to go was the Hyde Park service (6) in December 1961, though specials ran along it for Race Week in showers of sparks after a nine month lapse. This was followed by the Hexthorpe route (3) in March 1962, with Balby (10) going the same way in September of the same year. Thus was left the Wheatley Hills route (4) abandoned in December 1962, Race Course (6), on which No. 377 ran as last vehicles in October 1963 and, last of all, Beckett Road (5) on 14th December 1963, when the last vehicle, No. 375 made the final run with local dignitaries and enthusiasts on board. This vehicle was eventually preserved by the Doncaster Omnibus & Light Railway Society. Out of service but available at the depot on the last day were also Nos. 369, 376 and 377 which were broken up in February 1964.

It was decided to refit a batch of trolleybus bodies on to motor bus chassis in 1964, on new Daimler CVG 6 chassis, with pleasing though not entirely successful results as the appearance tended to be some-what heavy browed and ponderous. It was, however, a cheap and painless transition from one mode of propulsion to another.

37

Withdrawal dates of the vehicles in trolleybus guise was as follows:

384 (169) 31.12.61	390 (183) 27.9.62
385 (184) 5.9.62	391 (182) 22.7.62
386 (168) 28.11.61	392 (173)13.6.62
387 (185) 17.9.62	351 (170)1962/3.
388/9 (187/6) 28.9.62	352 (171) 1962/3

The new fleet numbers are in brackets. A last batch of trolley vehicle conversions took place firstly when Nos. 394 and 395, withdrawn on 28.2.63 and 31.12.62 respectively gained Leyland PD2/40 chassis and Nos. 189 and 188, following which the others were given PD2/1 chassis and new numbers as follows:

393	(94)	withdrawn as trolleybus	10.03.63
396	(93)	' '	31.12.62
397	(95)	' '	'
398	(96)	' '	'
353	(124)	' '	1962/3
354	(123)	' '	'

Thus the shades of the old trolley vehicles lingered on, masquerading in the guise of motor vehicles which, though efficient, did not look quite right, like an older lady in a young girl's wig. At least they were more acceptable than the well advertised 'gearless' buses which used to ply earlier in the Company's history, starting away from a stop with an almighty roaring sound which could frighten all around.

One man vehicles now appear universally, swifter but noisier than the older electric transport. Maroon has given way to weak tea and cream with a dash of red under the aegis of South Yorkshire Passenger Transport Executive, with the often glimpsed liveries of private operators.

Flowery comment on the new tramway system by the reporter for the Doncaster Chronicle, written on 30th May 1902:

'The Tramways are chiefly in evidence at the present moment; locally they are the new attraction added to the show. Journeys have already been made, mostly nocturnal, to Hexthorpe and Balby, and prudent gentlemen of age and experience have been found to adventure themselves on a new and untried track, with electrical terrors untold above and beneath them. These have been experimental trips demanding resolution and fortitude from those officially connected with the undertaking, and we are glad to learn that, notwithstanding some recent and disturbing tram-car accidents at Scarborough, Liverpool and elsewhere, members of the Town Council and others were found courageous enough to encounter the perils of the unknown. What gave rise to no little surprise, no doubt, was the deadening fact that hundreds and even thousands of people were looking on, all the while envying them and longing to be in their place! Nothing exceeds the crass insensibility of an unimaginative, not to say an unintelligent crowd! What a reflection for brave, desperate, devoted men! Happily, all returned in safety and the tramways have been now passed by the Government Inspector, so far as now completed and will be formally opened on Monday next, for which occasion the Mayor has issued invitations to a luncheon at the Mansion House. From that day, it may be expected, the cars will be set regularly running to Balby and Hexthorpe, every quarter of an hour or so. Meanwhile, the stopping places are being marked out and indicated: for these cars are not stopped, as a rule, as one stops an omnibus, but have their regular stages-the halting places being indicated by a white or coloured band on the post or standard. We must certainly congratulate the Corporation, and more particularly the special committee, on the class of car they have adopted-they have shown no false economy but have purchased really handsome and thoroughly well-built coaches. These are indeed among the best that we have seen, and we are speaking from a pretty fair experience of the latest developments in this direction. Each car is a capacious, well upholstered, admirably fitted saloon in itself-lighted in the daytime by six, large plate glass windows, three a side, and, at night-time, by six electric lamps. The seats are comfortable curved and warmly rugged, and there are call-bells overhead easily reached by the passengers. The grainwork and decorations are exceedingly neat, and nothing is left to be desired by the ordinary 'fare', save the assurance from his neighbours that 'it all pays'. The cars are constructed to carry 56 passengers, 24 inside and 32 outside, the light seats on the roof adding but little to the total weight of the car. A warm tone of maroon has been chosen for the body of the carriages, which are finely varnished and 'brought up', the Doncaster arms and motto being prettily emblazoned in the centre on both sides. The upper parts and under carriage are finished in pale yellow, the latter bearing the inscription 'Doncaster Corporation Tramways'. Large, flat crystal discs occupy the very centre of each end and, when lighted, thoroughly illuminate the track for some distance ahead; above, over the head of the driver and conductor are letter-perforated screens or plates, which by day or night plainly indicate the destination of any particular car, whilst a small coloured disc, fore and aft, will tell at a distance whether it Balby or Bentley, Hexthorpe or Hyde Park the car is going to; each district and has its own colour. The whole equipment is very satisfactory, and nothing more so, apparently, than the ingenious provision made for preventing those knocked down being run over by these cars. It is a late and ingenious invention, approved by the Board of Trade. A light framework runs in front immediately under the driver's platform, and the instant this touches a body or an obstacle, a large tray or staging is dropped a foot or two behind in advance of the wheels and close to the ground. In the case of a child or adult, dog or sheep this tray would receive the body and carry it forward free of the metals. Such at least is the invention in theory; possibly its practical value will be soon tested, as all manner of accidents are being predicted for Doncaster's last new 'plaything'.

Types of vehicle available during 1923-1963

Year,	Trams	S/deck buses.	D/deck buses.	Trolleybuses.
1923	47	6		
1924	47	12		
1925	47	13	2	
1926	47	13	4	
1927	44	14	7	
1928	38	17	7	
1929	38	20	8	16
1930	18	31	8	22
1931	14	34	8	30
1932	11	34	8	31
1933	9	28	10	31
1934	9	26	12	32
1935	9	22	14	32
1936		22	14	37
1937		22	16	39
1938		26	21	38
1939		25	24	39
1940		24	25	44
1941		22	27	44
1942		26	27	44
1943		26	31	44
1944		25	37	45
1945		21	35	45
1946		19	36	46
1947		19	38	46
1948		18	46	46
1949		17	48	46
1950		14	53	46
1951		14	5	46
1952		14	51	46
1953		11	51	46
1954		11	53	44
1955		11	55	42
1956		11	66	34
1957		7	66	34
1958		7	69	34
1953		7	70	34
1960		7	74	28
1961		7	74	28
1962		10	73	25
1963		10	90	14

Routes and Mileages

Date Route Opened (trams)		Date of Conversion to Trolleybuses	Final Closure	Mileage
Balby	2.6.1902	26.7.31	9.9.62	2.25
Hexthorpe	2.6.1902	1.7.29	18.3.92	1.22
Race Course	30.6.1902	20.3.30	14.10.63	2.90
Hyde Park	1.8.1902	16.1.30	11.12.61	2.90
Bentley	27.10.1902	22.8.28	13.2.56	2.70
Avenue Road	15.1.19.3	4.3.31	31.12.62	2.40*
Beckett Road	17.8.1903	31.7.29	14.10.63	2.01
Oxford Street	25.11.1903	-		
Brodsworth	21.2.1916	-		

* as Wheatley Hills Route

More Facts

The new bus stand at North Bridge cost £6,114.
Cost of the first eight Trolleybuses was £2,105 each.
Trolleybuses running costs were latterly £8,000 to £11,000 per week.
Unlimited bus passes were introduced on 23.8.1923, to deter pirate operators.
From 6.32 these gave unlimited rides on weekdays only.
From 10.41 passes offered 24 rides per week.

On the Balby route, the old Oswin Avenue terminus was used for short workings by trams at busy times. Pointwork throughout the system was changed by the conductor using an iron for the rails and a stirrup on the post for the overhead. A trolley reverser was fitted at the Warmsworth terminus, the only one on the system.

Trolleybus No.1 was used for crew training during 1928 and for a time in 1938.

No. 385 came to grief on a late run when it collided with a single decker bus at the junction of Cleveland Street and Spring Gardens on 25th April 1958. No serious injuries resulted, though the vehicle was thrown on to its nearside. It was returned to service in due course.

At Playfair's Corner on the Bentley route a section of wiring was put in to allow short workings from town to reverse at a point where the out and home routes divided to run round the houses. A similar section of wiring was put in latterly to enable vehicles to run into West Laith Gate from St. Sepulchre Gate under their own power.

The run to and from Hexthorpe took ten minutes, while that to Bentley took half an hour; 5 vehicles were used during the week, with 6 on Saturdays.

The first Electrical & Tramway Manager was Mr. E.S.Rayner, while the Traffic Superintendent was Mr. A.E.Blower. Early Inspectors were R. Cook and J.W.Saunders. In spite of quite a deal of enquiry, little has surfaced about the life of Mr. Tommy Potts, who was Transport Manager for most of the DCT's existence. We know that he retired in 1953 and that he wrote an article on the DCT system for 'Buses Illustrated' some time later. Mr. Geoffrey Oates has kindly written to say that Mr. Potts lived opposite to him in Norborough Road, Wheatley, a reclusive bachelor with his sister who outlived him and went to a Home at Burghwallis, where she died.

Now this is written, I shall have a belated flood of information, as often happens in such cases - keep writing!

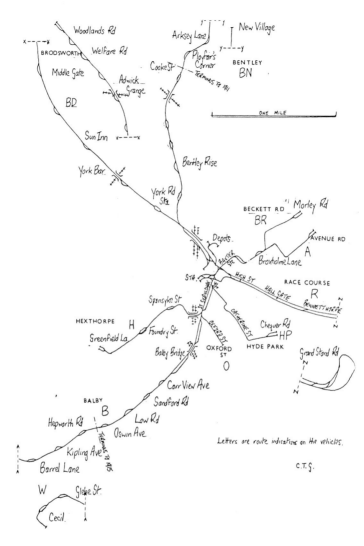

The Tramway system

Doncaster Transport crest up to 1975

Opposite: Ex GC 4•6•0 Clan B4 No 6099 leaves the Cattle Dock sidings at Doncaster station with a vintage GN triplet articulated set. This view, taken from the north end of the station, also shows a Gresley A1 Pacific approaching, admired by a young spotter (female), with the electricity works chimney in the background and two trolleybuses on North Bridge.
T. Rounthwaite

Other publications by the Author:

(* denotes those that are out of print but
which may be in stock or available in libraries.)

'The Mexborough & Swinton Traction Company.'*

'The Burton & Ashby Light Railway.'

'Railways in South Yorkshire.'*

'Railways of North Lincs.'

'The Wakefield, Pontefract & Goole Railway.'

'The Railways of Castleford.'

'Huddersfield Branch Lines.'

'The Railways of Hull.'

'The Selby & Driffield Railway.'

'To the Crystal Palace.' (Forge Books)

'To the Alexandra Palace.' (Forge Books)